90-Day
Mood Tracking
Journal

Track your Mood, Sleep, Energy, Food, Goals & more

Disclaimer

Disclaimer: The content within this book is designed to aid in monitoring moods and emotions it is not intended for the diagnosis or treatment of any medical conditions.

A Note from the Author

Aloha to all my Ohana!

Thank you for purchasing my 90-Day Mood Tracker Journal.

I am so excited and delighted to share with you, a project which I have been working on for some time.

These past three years have been a roller-coaster ride! Trying to conceive and start a family, having three difficult pregnancies, COVID-19, the pandemic, and raising two children under the age of 3, it's been emotionally and physically draining. I remember going to my postpartum doctor's appointments and my doctor asking me questions about my eating habits and sleep. As a first-time mother, I would stare with a blank face because I couldn't even remember what day it was, let alone what my blood pressure was 3 days ago.

This is why I created this helpful resource to help you monitor these important questions.

The 90-Day Mood Tracker Journal has two parts. The tracker section is used to monitor sleep, food, mood, energy, blood pressure, etc. Included in the tracker section is a journal or notes area, it's a great way to reflect on your day. The next section has positive, mood-tracking journal prompts that give insights into understanding your mood, how your mood has progressed, and what steps you can take to better it.

This journal can be used:

- ✓ If you are in ANY type of recovery
- ✓ Managing stress or anxiety
- ✓ Need to monitor daily medications and blood pressure
- ✓ Bettering your mental health and more

Thank you for allowing me to help in your journey of self-realization, self-reflection, and most importantly, self-love!

Mahalo,

K Petit

How to use this book

Fill in daily to track trends in your moods and identify triggers

Date: ________________ Day M T W T F S S

Hours of Sleep: _______________

Mood (Morning)

Evening (Morning)

Water Intake	Energy Level

Did you feel any of the following today?

☐ Energized	☐ Happy	☐ Motivated	☐ Excited
☐ Sad	☐ Upset	☐ Lost	☐ Angry
☐ Optimistic	☐ Creative	☐ Joyful	☐ Productive
☐ Bored	☐ Annoyed	☐ Confused	☐ Hesitant

Food Intake

Breakfast	Lunch	Dinner	Snacks

Blood Pressure Chart

Time	Systolic (Upper)	Diastolic (Lower)	Heart Rate

Medications

Three Goals for Today...

Notes

1. ____

2. ____

3. ____

What impacted your mood today?

What activities or people brought positivity to your day?

What thoughts or events made you feel anxious or upset today?

How did you cope with those feelings?

Did you practice self-care today? If not, what self-care activities can you plan for tomorrow?

Date: _______________   Day   M   T   W   T   F   S   S

Hours of Sleep: _______________

| Water Intake | Energy Level |

Mood (Morning)

Evening (Morning)

Did you feel any of the following today?

☐	Energized	☐	Happy	☐	Motivated	☐	Excited
☐	Sad	☐	Upset	☐	Lost	☐	Angry
☐	Optimistic	☐	Creative	☐	Joyful	☐	Productive
☐	Bored	☐	Annoyed	☐	Confused	☐	Hesitant

Food Intake

Breakfast	Lunch	Dinner	Snacks

Blood Pressure Chart

Time	Systolic (Upper)	Diastolic (Lower)	Heart Rate

Medications

Three Goals for Today...

1. _______________________________

2. _______________________________

3. _______________________________

Notes

What impacted your mood today?

What activities or people brought positivity to your day?

What thoughts or events made you feel anxious or upset today?

How did you cope with those feelings?

Did you practice self-care today? If not, what self-care activities can you plan for tomorrow?

Date: _______________   Day   M   T   W   T   F   S   S

Hours of Sleep: _______________

| Water Intake | Energy Level |

Mood (Morning)

Evening (Morning)

Did you feel any of the following today?

- Energized
- Happy
- Motivated
- Excited
- Sad
- Upset
- Lost
- Angry
- Optimistic
- Creative
- Joyful
- Productive
- Bored
- Annoyed
- Confused
- Hesitant

Food Intake

Breakfast	Lunch	Dinner	Snacks

Blood Pressure Chart

Time	Systolic (Upper)	Diastolic (Lower)	Heart Rate

Medications

Three Goals for Today...

1. _______________________________

2. _______________________________

3. _______________________________

Notes

What impacted your mood today?

What activities or people brought positivity to your day?

What thoughts or events made you feel anxious or upset today?

How did you cope with those feelings?

Did you practice self-care today? If not, what self-care activities can you plan for tomorrow?

Date: __________   Day   M   T   W   T   F   S   S

Hours of Sleep: __________

Mood (Morning)

😀 🙂 😐 🙁 😠

Evening (Morning)

😀 🙂 😐 🙁 😠

Water Intake	Energy Level

Did you feel any of the following today?

- [ ] Energized
- [ ] Happy
- [ ] Motivated
- [ ] Excited
- [ ] Sad
- [ ] Upset
- [ ] Lost
- [ ] Angry
- [ ] Optimistic
- [ ] Creative
- [ ] Joyful
- [ ] Productive
- [ ] Bored
- [ ] Annoyed
- [ ] Confused
- [ ] Hesitant

Food Intake

Breakfast	Lunch	Dinner	Snacks

Blood Pressure Chart

Time	Systolic (Upper)	Diastolic (Lower)	Heart Rate

Medications

Three Goals for Today...

1. ____________________

2. ____________________

3. ____________________

Notes

What impacted your mood today?

What activities or people brought positivity to your day?

What thoughts or events made you feel anxious or upset today?

How did you cope with those feelings?

Did you practice self-care today? If not, what self-care activities can you plan for tomorrow?

Date: _____________   Day   M   T   W   T   F   S   S

Hours of Sleep: _____________

| Water Intake | Energy Level |

Mood (Morning)

Evening (Morning)

Did you feel any of the following today?

- [ ] Energized
- [ ] Happy
- [ ] Motivated
- [ ] Excited
- [ ] Sad
- [ ] Upset
- [ ] Lost
- [ ] Angry
- [ ] Optimistic
- [ ] Creative
- [ ] Joyful
- [ ] Productive
- [ ] Bored
- [ ] Annoyed
- [ ] Confused
- [ ] Hesitant

Food Intake

Breakfast	Lunch	Dinner	Snacks

Blood Pressure Chart

Time	Systolic (Upper)	Diastolic (Lower)	Heart Rate

Medications

Three Goals for Today...   Notes

1. _______________________

2. _______________________

3. _______________________

What impacted your mood today?

What activities or people brought positivity to your day?

What thoughts or events made you feel anxious or upset today?

How did you cope with those feelings?

Did you practice self-care today? If not, what self-care activities can you plan for tomorrow?

Date: _____________   Day   M   T   W   T   F   S   S

Hours of Sleep: _____________

Mood (Morning)

Evening (Morning)

Water Intake

Energy Level

Did you feel any of the following today?

- [ ] Energized
- [ ] Happy
- [ ] Motivated
- [ ] Excited
- [ ] Sad
- [ ] Upset
- [ ] Lost
- [ ] Angry
- [ ] Optimistic
- [ ] Creative
- [ ] Joyful
- [ ] Productive
- [ ] Bored
- [ ] Annoyed
- [ ] Confused
- [ ] Hesitant

Food Intake

Breakfast	Lunch	Dinner	Snacks

Blood Pressure Chart

Time	Systolic (Upper)	Diastolic (Lower)	Heart Rate

Medications

Three Goals for Today...

Notes

1. _______________________________

2. _______________________________

3. _______________________________

What impacted your mood today?

What activities or people brought positivity to your day?

What thoughts or events made you feel anxious or upset today?

How did you cope with those feelings?

Did you practice self-care today? If not, what self-care activities can you plan for tomorrow?

Date: __________   Day   M   T   W   T   F   S   S

Hours of Sleep: __________

Mood (Morning)

Evening (Morning)

Water Intake	Energy Level

Did you feel any of the following today?

- [ ] Energized
- [ ] Happy
- [ ] Motivated
- [ ] Excited
- [ ] Sad
- [ ] Upset
- [ ] Lost
- [ ] Angry
- [ ] Optimistic
- [ ] Creative
- [ ] Joyful
- [ ] Productive
- [ ] Bored
- [ ] Annoyed
- [ ] Confused
- [ ] Hesitant

Food Intake

Breakfast	Lunch	Dinner	Snacks

Blood Pressure Chart

Time	Systolic (Upper)	Diastolic (Lower)	Heart Rate

Medications

Three Goals for Today...

Notes

1. __________

2. __________

3. __________

What impacted your mood today?

What activities or people brought positivity to your day?

What thoughts or events made you feel anxious or upset today?

How did you cope with those feelings?

Did you practice self-care today? If not, what self-care activities can you plan for tomorrow?

Date: _____________   Day   M   T   W   T   F   S   S

Hours of Sleep: _____________

Mood (Morning)

Evening (Morning)

Water Intake

Energy Level

Did you feel any of the following today?

- ☐ Energized
- ☐ Happy
- ☐ Motivated
- ☐ Excited
- ☐ Sad
- ☐ Upset
- ☐ Lost
- ☐ Angry
- ☐ Optimistic
- ☐ Creative
- ☐ Joyful
- ☐ Productive
- ☐ Bored
- ☐ Annoyed
- ☐ Confused
- ☐ Hesitant

Food Intake

Breakfast	Lunch	Dinner	Snacks

Blood Pressure Chart

Time	Systolic (Upper)	Diastolic (Lower)	Heart Rate

Medications

Three Goals for Today...

1.
2.
3.

Notes

What impacted your mood today?

What activities or people brought positivity to your day?

What thoughts or events made you feel anxious or upset today?

How did you cope with those feelings?

Did you practice self-care today? If not, what self-care activities can you plan for tomorrow?

Date: _____________   Day   M   T   W   T   F   S   S

Hours of Sleep: _____________

Water Intake	Energy Level

Did you feel any of the following today?

- [ ] Energized
- [ ] Happy
- [ ] Motivated
- [ ] Excited
- [ ] Sad
- [ ] Upset
- [ ] Lost
- [ ] Angry
- [ ] Optimistic
- [ ] Creative
- [ ] Joyful
- [ ] Productive
- [ ] Bored
- [ ] Annoyed
- [ ] Confused
- [ ] Hesitant

Food Intake

Breakfast	Lunch	Dinner	Snacks

Blood Pressure Chart

Time	Systolic (Upper)	Diastolic (Lower)	Heart Rate

Medications

Three Goals for Today...   Notes

1. _____________________________

2. _____________________________

3. _____________________________

What impacted your mood today?

What activities or people brought positivity to your day?

What thoughts or events made you feel anxious or upset today?

How did you cope with those feelings?

Did you practice self-care today? If not, what self-care activities can you plan for tomorrow?

Date: _____________   Day   M   T   W   T   F   S   S

Hours of Sleep: _____________

Mood (Morning)

Evening (Morning)

Water Intake	Energy Level

Did you feel any of the following today?

☐ Energized	☐ Happy	☐ Motivated	☐ Excited
☐ Sad	☐ Upset	☐ Lost	☐ Angry
☐ Optimistic	☐ Creative	☐ Joyful	☐ Productive
☐ Bored	☐ Annoyed	☐ Confused	☐ Hesitant

Food Intake

Breakfast	Lunch	Dinner	Snacks

Blood Pressure Chart

Time	Systolic (Upper)	Diastolic (Lower)	Heart Rate

Medications

Three Goals for Today…

1. _______________________

2. _______________________

3. _______________________

Notes

What impacted your mood today?

What activities or people brought positivity to your day?

What thoughts or events made you feel anxious or upset today?

How did you cope with those feelings?

Did you practice self-care today? If not, what self-care activities can you plan for tomorrow?

Date: _____________   Day   M   T   W   T   F   S   S

Hours of Sleep: _____________

Mood (Morning)

Evening (Morning)

| Water Intake | Energy Level |

Did you feel any of the following today?

- [ ] Energized
- [ ] Happy
- [ ] Motivated
- [ ] Excited
- [ ] Sad
- [ ] Upset
- [ ] Lost
- [ ] Angry
- [ ] Optimistic
- [ ] Creative
- [ ] Joyful
- [ ] Productive
- [ ] Bored
- [ ] Annoyed
- [ ] Confused
- [ ] Hesitant

Food Intake

Breakfast	Lunch	Dinner	Snacks

Blood Pressure Chart

Time	Systolic (Upper)	Diastolic (Lower)	Heart Rate

Medications

Three Goals for Today...

1.

2.

3.

Notes

What impacted your mood today?

What activities or people brought positivity to your day?

What thoughts or events made you feel anxious or upset today?

How did you cope with those feelings?

Did you practice self-care today? If not, what self-care activities can you plan for tomorrow?

Date: _____________   Day   M   T   W   T   F   S   S

Hours of Sleep: _____________

| Water Intake | Energy Level |

Mood (Morning)

☺ ☺ 😐 ☹ 😠

Evening (Morning)

☺ ☺ 😐 ☹ 😠

Did you feel any of the following today?

☐ Energized	☐ Happy	☐ Motivated	☐ Excited
☐ Sad	☐ Upset	☐ Lost	☐ Angry
☐ Optimistic	☐ Creative	☐ Joyful	☐ Productive
☐ Bored	☐ Annoyed	☐ Confused	☐ Hesitant

Food Intake

Breakfast	Lunch	Dinner	Snacks

Blood Pressure Chart

Time	Systolic (Upper)	Diastolic (Lower)	Heart Rate

Medications

Three Goals for Today...   Notes

1. ___________________________

2. ___________________________

3. ___________________________

What impacted your mood today?

What activities or people brought positivity to your day?

What thoughts or events made you feel anxious or upset today?

How did you cope with those feelings?

Did you practice self-care today? If not, what self-care activities can you plan for tomorrow?

Date: ___________   Day   M   T   W   T   F   S   S

Hours of Sleep: ___________

Mood (Morning)

Evening (Morning)

Water Intake

Energy Level

Did you feel any of the following today?

- [ ] Energized
- [ ] Happy
- [ ] Motivated
- [ ] Excited
- [ ] Sad
- [ ] Upset
- [ ] Lost
- [ ] Angry
- [ ] Optimistic
- [ ] Creative
- [ ] Joyful
- [ ] Productive
- [ ] Bored
- [ ] Annoyed
- [ ] Confused
- [ ] Hesitant

Food Intake

Breakfast	Lunch	Dinner	Snacks

Blood Pressure Chart

Time	Systolic (Upper)	Diastolic (Lower)	Heart Rate

Medications

Three Goals for Today...

1.

2.

3.

Notes

What impacted your mood today?

What activities or people brought positivity to your day?

What thoughts or events made you feel anxious or upset today?

How did you cope with those feelings?

Did you practice self-care today? If not, what self-care activities can you plan for tomorrow?

Date: __________   Day   M   T   W   T   F   S   S

Hours of Sleep: __________

Mood (Morning)

Evening (Morning)

| Water Intake | Energy Level |

Did you feel any of the following today?

- [ ] Energized
- [ ] Happy
- [ ] Motivated
- [ ] Excited
- [ ] Sad
- [ ] Upset
- [ ] Lost
- [ ] Angry
- [ ] Optimistic
- [ ] Creative
- [ ] Joyful
- [ ] Productive
- [ ] Bored
- [ ] Annoyed
- [ ] Confused
- [ ] Hesitant

Food Intake

Breakfast	Lunch	Dinner	Snacks

Blood Pressure Chart

Time	Systolic (Upper)	Diastolic (Lower)	Heart Rate

Medications

Three Goals for Today...

Notes

1. __________

2. __________

3. __________

What impacted your mood today?

What activities or people brought positivity to your day?

What thoughts or events made you feel anxious or upset today?

How did you cope with those feelings?

Did you practice self-care today? If not, what self-care activities can you plan for tomorrow?

Date: ___________ Day   M   T   W   T   F   S   S

Hours of Sleep: ___________

Mood (Morning)

Evening (Morning)

Water Intake	Energy Level

Did you feel any of the following today?

☐ Energized	☐ Happy	☐ Motivated	☐ Excited
☐ Sad	☐ Upset	☐ Lost	☐ Angry
☐ Optimistic	☐ Creative	☐ Joyful	☐ Productive
☐ Bored	☐ Annoyed	☐ Confused	☐ Hesitant

Food Intake

Breakfast	Lunch	Dinner	Snacks

Blood Pressure Chart

Time	Systolic (Upper)	Diastolic (Lower)	Heart Rate

Medications

Three Goals for Today...

1.

2.

3.

Notes

What impacted your mood today?

What activities or people brought positivity to your day?

What thoughts or events made you feel anxious or upset today?

How did you cope with those feelings?

Did you practice self-care today? If not, what self-care activities can you plan for tomorrow?

Date: __________   Day   M   T   W   T   F   S   S

Hours of Sleep: __________

Mood (Morning)

😄 🙂 😐 🙁 😠

Evening (Morning)

😄 🙂 😐 🙁 😠

Water Intake	Energy Level

Did you feel any of the following today?

- ☐ Energized
- ☐ Happy
- ☐ Motivated
- ☐ Excited
- ☐ Sad
- ☐ Upset
- ☐ Lost
- ☐ Angry
- ☐ Optimistic
- ☐ Creative
- ☐ Joyful
- ☐ Productive
- ☐ Bored
- ☐ Annoyed
- ☐ Confused
- ☐ Hesitant

Food Intake

Breakfast	Lunch	Dinner	Snacks

Blood Pressure Chart

Time	Systolic (Upper)	Diastolic (Lower)	Heart Rate

Medications

Three Goals for Today...

Notes

1. ______________________________

2. ______________________________

3. ______________________________

What impacted your mood today?

What activities or people brought positivity to your day?

What thoughts or events made you feel anxious or upset today?

How did you cope with those feelings?

Did you practice self-care today? If not, what self-care activities can you plan for tomorrow?

Date: ___________   Day   M   T   W   T   F   S   S

Hours of Sleep: ___________

Mood (Morning)

Evening (Morning)

Water Intake

Energy Level

Did you feel any of the following today?

- [ ] Energized
- [ ] Happy
- [ ] Motivated
- [ ] Excited
- [ ] Sad
- [ ] Upset
- [ ] Lost
- [ ] Angry
- [ ] Optimistic
- [ ] Creative
- [ ] Joyful
- [ ] Productive
- [ ] Bored
- [ ] Annoyed
- [ ] Confused
- [ ] Hesitant

Food Intake

Breakfast	Lunch	Dinner	Snacks

Blood Pressure Chart

Time	Systolic (Upper)	Diastolic (Lower)	Heart Rate

Medications

Three Goals for Today...   Notes

1. ______________________

2. ______________________

3. ______________________

What impacted your mood today?

What activities or people brought positivity to your day?

What thoughts or events made you feel anxious or upset today?

How did you cope with those feelings?

Did you practice self-care today? If not, what self-care activities can you plan for tomorrow?

Date: _____________ Day   M   T   W   T   F   S   S

Hours of Sleep: _____________

Mood (Morning)

Evening (Morning)

Water Intake | Energy Level

Did you feel any of the following today?

- [ ] Energized
- [ ] Happy
- [ ] Motivated
- [ ] Excited
- [ ] Sad
- [ ] Upset
- [ ] Lost
- [ ] Angry
- [ ] Optimistic
- [ ] Creative
- [ ] Joyful
- [ ] Productive
- [ ] Bored
- [ ] Annoyed
- [ ] Confused
- [ ] Hesitant

Food Intake

Breakfast	Lunch	Dinner	Snacks

Blood Pressure Chart

Time	Systolic (Upper)	Diastolic (Lower)	Heart Rate

Medications

Three Goals for Today...

Notes

1. _______________________________

2. _______________________________

3. _______________________________

What impacted your mood today?

What activities or people brought positivity to your day?

What thoughts or events made you feel anxious or upset today?

How did you cope with those feelings?

Did you practice self-care today? If not, what self-care activities can you plan for tomorrow?

Date: ____________ Day M T W T F S S

Hours of Sleep: ____________

Mood (Morning)

Evening (Morning)

Water Intake	Energy Level

Did you feel any of the following today?

- [ ] Energized
- [ ] Happy
- [ ] Motivated
- [ ] Excited
- [ ] Sad
- [ ] Upset
- [ ] Lost
- [ ] Angry
- [ ] Optimistic
- [ ] Creative
- [ ] Joyful
- [ ] Productive
- [ ] Bored
- [ ] Annoyed
- [ ] Confused
- [ ] Hesitant

Food Intake

Breakfast	Lunch	Dinner	Snacks

Blood Pressure Chart

Time	Systolic (Upper)	Diastolic (Lower)	Heart Rate

Medications

Three Goals for Today...

1. _________________________

2. _________________________

3. _________________________

Notes

What impacted your mood today?

What activities or people brought positivity to your day?

What thoughts or events made you feel anxious or upset today?

How did you cope with those feelings?

Did you practice self-care today? If not, what self-care activities can you plan for tomorrow?

Date: __________   Day   M   T   W   T   F   S   S

Hours of Sleep: __________

Mood (Morning)

Evening (Morning)

Water Intake	Energy Level

Did you feel any of the following today?

- [ ] Energized
- [ ] Happy
- [ ] Motivated
- [ ] Excited
- [ ] Sad
- [ ] Upset
- [ ] Lost
- [ ] Angry
- [ ] Optimistic
- [ ] Creative
- [ ] Joyful
- [ ] Productive
- [ ] Bored
- [ ] Annoyed
- [ ] Confused
- [ ] Hesitant

Food Intake

Breakfast	Lunch	Dinner	Snacks

Blood Pressure Chart

Time	Systolic (Upper)	Diastolic (Lower)	Heart Rate

Medications

Three Goals for Today...

1.

2.

3.

Notes

What impacted your mood today?

What activities or people brought positivity to your day?

What thoughts or events made you feel anxious or upset today?

How did you cope with those feelings?

Did you practice self-care today? If not, what self-care activities can you plan for tomorrow?

Date: _______________   Day   M   T   W   T   F   S   S

Hours of Sleep: _______________

Water Intake	Energy Level

Mood (Morning)

Evening (Morning)

Did you feel any of the following today?

- ☐ Energized
- ☐ Happy
- ☐ Motivated
- ☐ Excited
- ☐ Sad
- ☐ Upset
- ☐ Lost
- ☐ Angry
- ☐ Optimistic
- ☐ Creative
- ☐ Joyful
- ☐ Productive
- ☐ Bored
- ☐ Annoyed
- ☐ Confused
- ☐ Hesitant

Food Intake

Breakfast	Lunch	Dinner	Snacks

Blood Pressure Chart

Time	Systolic (Upper)	Diastolic (Lower)	Heart Rate

Medications

Three Goals for Today...

1. _______________

2. _______________

3. _______________

Notes

What impacted your mood today?

What activities or people brought positivity to your day?

What thoughts or events made you feel anxious or upset today?

How did you cope with those feelings?

Did you practice self-care today? If not, what self-care activities can you plan for tomorrow?

Date: __________   Day   M   T   W   T   F   S   S

Hours of Sleep: __________

Mood (Morning)

Evening (Morning)

Water Intake

Energy Level

Did you feel any of the following today?

☐ Energized	☐ Happy	☐ Motivated	☐ Excited
☐ Sad	☐ Upset	☐ Lost	☐ Angry
☐ Optimistic	☐ Creative	☐ Joyful	☐ Productive
☐ Bored	☐ Annoyed	☐ Confused	☐ Hesitant

Food Intake

Breakfast	Lunch	Dinner	Snacks

Blood Pressure Chart

Time	Systolic (Upper)	Diastolic (Lower)	Heart Rate

Medications

Three Goals for Today...

1.

2.

3.

Notes

What impacted your mood today?

What activities or people brought positivity to your day?

What thoughts or events made you feel anxious or upset today?

How did you cope with those feelings?

Did you practice self-care today? If not, what self-care activities can you plan for tomorrow?

Date: _______________   Day   M   T   W   T   F   S   S

Hours of Sleep: _______________

| Water Intake | Energy Level |

Mood (Morning)

Evening (Morning)

Did you feel any of the following today?

- [ ] Energized
- [ ] Happy
- [ ] Motivated
- [ ] Excited
- [ ] Sad
- [ ] Upset
- [ ] Lost
- [ ] Angry
- [ ] Optimistic
- [ ] Creative
- [ ] Joyful
- [ ] Productive
- [ ] Bored
- [ ] Annoyed
- [ ] Confused
- [ ] Hesitant

Food Intake

Breakfast	Lunch	Dinner	Snacks

Blood Pressure Chart

Time	Systolic (Upper)	Diastolic (Lower)	Heart Rate

Medications

Three Goals for Today...   Notes

1. ______________________________

2. ______________________________

3. ______________________________

What impacted your mood today?

What activities or people brought positivity to your day?

What thoughts or events made you feel anxious or upset today?

How did you cope with those feelings?

Did you practice self-care today? If not, what self-care activities can you plan for tomorrow?

Date: _____________ Day   M   T   W   T   F   S   S

Hours of Sleep: _____________

Mood (Morning)

Evening (Morning)

Water Intake	Energy Level

Did you feel any of the following today?

- [ ] Energized
- [ ] Happy
- [ ] Motivated
- [ ] Excited
- [ ] Sad
- [ ] Upset
- [ ] Lost
- [ ] Angry
- [ ] Optimistic
- [ ] Creative
- [ ] Joyful
- [ ] Productive
- [ ] Bored
- [ ] Annoyed
- [ ] Confused
- [ ] Hesitant

Food Intake

Breakfast	Lunch	Dinner	Snacks

Blood Pressure Chart

Time	Systolic (Upper)	Diastolic (Lower)	Heart Rate

Medications

Three Goals for Today...

1. ______________________________

2. ______________________________

3. ______________________________

Notes

What impacted your mood today?

What activities or people brought positivity to your day?

What thoughts or events made you feel anxious or upset today?

How did you cope with those feelings?

Did you practice self-care today? If not, what self-care activities can
you plan for tomorrow?

Date: _____________   Day   M   T   W   T   F   S   S

Hours of Sleep: _____________

Mood (Morning)

Evening (Morning)

| Water Intake | Energy Level |

Did you feel any of the following today?

- [ ] Energized
- [ ] Happy
- [ ] Motivated
- [ ] Excited
- [ ] Sad
- [ ] Upset
- [ ] Lost
- [ ] Angry
- [ ] Optimistic
- [ ] Creative
- [ ] Joyful
- [ ] Productive
- [ ] Bored
- [ ] Annoyed
- [ ] Confused
- [ ] Hesitant

Food Intake

Breakfast	Lunch	Dinner	Snacks

Blood Pressure Chart

Time	Systolic (Upper)	Diastolic (Lower)	Heart Rate

Medications

Three Goals for Today...

1.

2.

3.

Notes

What impacted your mood today?

What activities or people brought positivity to your day?

What thoughts or events made you feel anxious or upset today?

How did you cope with those feelings?

Did you practice self-care today? If not, what self-care activities can you plan for tomorrow?

Date: _____________   Day   M   T   W   T   F   S   S

Hours of Sleep: _____________

Water Intake	Energy Level

Mood (Morning)

Evening (Morning)

Did you feel any of the following today?

- [ ] Energized
- [ ] Happy
- [ ] Motivated
- [ ] Excited
- [ ] Sad
- [ ] Upset
- [ ] Lost
- [ ] Angry
- [ ] Optimistic
- [ ] Creative
- [ ] Joyful
- [ ] Productive
- [ ] Bored
- [ ] Annoyed
- [ ] Confused
- [ ] Hesitant

Food Intake

Breakfast	Lunch	Dinner	Snacks

Blood Pressure Chart

Time	Systolic (Upper)	Diastolic (Lower)	Heart Rate

Medications

Three Goals for Today...   Notes

1. _______________________________

2. _______________________________

3. _______________________________

What impacted your mood today?

What activities or people brought positivity to your day?

What thoughts or events made you feel anxious or upset today?

How did you cope with those feelings?

Did you practice self-care today? If not, what self-care activities can you plan for tomorrow?

Date: ______________ Day M T W T F S S

Hours of Sleep: ______________

Mood (Morning)

Evening (Morning)

Water Intake

Energy Level

Did you feel any of the following today?

- [ ] Energized
- [ ] Happy
- [ ] Motivated
- [ ] Excited
- [ ] Sad
- [ ] Upset
- [ ] Lost
- [ ] Angry
- [ ] Optimistic
- [ ] Creative
- [ ] Joyful
- [ ] Productive
- [ ] Bored
- [ ] Annoyed
- [ ] Confused
- [ ] Hesitant

Food Intake

Breakfast	Lunch	Dinner	Snacks

Blood Pressure Chart

Time	Systolic (Upper)	Diastolic (Lower)	Heart Rate

Medications

Three Goals for Today...

1.

2.

3.

Notes

What impacted your mood today?

What activities or people brought positivity to your day?

What thoughts or events made you feel anxious or upset today?

How did you cope with those feelings?

Did you practice self-care today? If not, what self-care activities can you plan for tomorrow?

Date: _______________   Day   M   T   W   T   F   S   S

Hours of Sleep: _______________

| Water Intake | Energy Level |

Mood (Morning)

Evening (Morning)

Did you feel any of the following today?

- [ ] Energized
- [ ] Happy
- [ ] Motivated
- [ ] Excited
- [ ] Sad
- [ ] Upset
- [ ] Lost
- [ ] Angry
- [ ] Optimistic
- [ ] Creative
- [ ] Joyful
- [ ] Productive
- [ ] Bored
- [ ] Annoyed
- [ ] Confused
- [ ] Hesitant

Food Intake

Breakfast	Lunch	Dinner	Snacks

Blood Pressure Chart

Time	Systolic (Upper)	Diastolic (Lower)	Heart Rate

Medications

Three Goals for Today...

Notes

1.

2.

3.

What impacted your mood today?

What activities or people brought positivity to your day?

What thoughts or events made you feel anxious or upset today?

How did you cope with those feelings?

Did you practice self-care today? If not, what self-care activities can you plan for tomorrow?

Date: ___________ Day M T W T F S S

Hours of Sleep: ___________

Mood (Morning)

Evening (Morning)

| Water Intake | Energy Level |

Did you feel any of the following today?

- [ ] Energized
- [ ] Happy
- [ ] Motivated
- [ ] Excited
- [ ] Sad
- [ ] Upset
- [ ] Lost
- [ ] Angry
- [ ] Optimistic
- [ ] Creative
- [ ] Joyful
- [ ] Productive
- [ ] Bored
- [ ] Annoyed
- [ ] Confused
- [ ] Hesitant

Food Intake

Breakfast	Lunch	Dinner	Snacks

Blood Pressure Chart

Time	Systolic (Upper)	Diastolic (Lower)	Heart Rate

Medications

Three Goals for Today...

Notes

1. _______________

2. _______________

3. _______________

What impacted your mood today?

What activities or people brought positivity to your day?

What thoughts or events made you feel anxious or upset today?

How did you cope with those feelings?

Did you practice self-care today? If not, what self-care activities can you plan for tomorrow?

Date: __________ Day   M   T   W   T   F   S   S

Hours of Sleep: __________

Mood (Morning)

Evening (Morning)

Water Intake	Energy Level

Did you feel any of the following today?

- [ ] Energized
- [ ] Happy
- [ ] Motivated
- [ ] Excited
- [ ] Sad
- [ ] Upset
- [ ] Lost
- [ ] Angry
- [ ] Optimistic
- [ ] Creative
- [ ] Joyful
- [ ] Productive
- [ ] Bored
- [ ] Annoyed
- [ ] Confused
- [ ] Hesitant

Food Intake

Breakfast	Lunch	Dinner	Snacks

Blood Pressure Chart

Time	Systolic (Upper)	Diastolic (Lower)	Heart Rate

Medications

Three Goals for Today...   Notes

1.

2.

3.

What impacted your mood today?

What activities or people brought positivity to your day?

What thoughts or events made you feel anxious or upset today?

How did you cope with those feelings?

Did you practice self-care today? If not, what self-care activities can you plan for tomorrow?

Date: _____________ Day M T W T F S S

Hours of Sleep: _____________

Mood (Morning)

Evening (Morning)

| Water Intake | Energy Level |

Did you feel any of the following today?

- ☐ Energized
- ☐ Happy
- ☐ Motivated
- ☐ Excited
- ☐ Sad
- ☐ Upset
- ☐ Lost
- ☐ Angry
- ☐ Optimistic
- ☐ Creative
- ☐ Joyful
- ☐ Productive
- ☐ Bored
- ☐ Annoyed
- ☐ Confused
- ☐ Hesitant

Food Intake

Breakfast	Lunch	Dinner	Snacks

Blood Pressure Chart

Time	Systolic (Upper)	Diastolic (Lower)	Heart Rate

Medications

Three Goals for Today...

1.

2.

3.

Notes

What impacted your mood today?

What activities or people brought positivity to your day?

What thoughts or events made you feel anxious or upset today?

How did you cope with those feelings?

Did you practice self-care today? If not, what self-care activities can you plan for tomorrow?

Date: _______________ Day M T W T F S S

Hours of Sleep: _______________

Mood (Morning)

Evening (Morning)

Water Intake

Energy Level

Did you feel any of the following today?

- Energized
- Happy
- Motivated
- Excited
- Sad
- Upset
- Lost
- Angry
- Optimistic
- Creative
- Joyful
- Productive
- Bored
- Annoyed
- Confused
- Hesitant

Food Intake

Breakfast	Lunch	Dinner	Snacks

Blood Pressure Chart

Time	Systolic (Upper)	Diastolic (Lower)	Heart Rate

Medications

Three Goals for Today...

1.

2.

3.

Notes

What impacted your mood today?

What activities or people brought positivity to your day?

What thoughts or events made you feel anxious or upset today?

How did you cope with those feelings?

Did you practice self-care today? If not, what self-care activities can you plan for tomorrow?

Date: _____________   Day   M   T   W   T   F   S   S

Hours of Sleep: _____________

Mood (Morning)

😃 🙂 😐 🙁 😠

Evening (Morning)

😃 🙂 😐 🙁 😠

Water Intake	Energy Level

Did you feel any of the following today?

☐ Energized	☐ Happy	☐ Motivated	☐ Excited
☐ Sad	☐ Upset	☐ Lost	☐ Angry
☐ Optimistic	☐ Creative	☐ Joyful	☐ Productive
☐ Bored	☐ Annoyed	☐ Confused	☐ Hesitant

Food Intake

Breakfast	Lunch	Dinner	Snacks

Blood Pressure Chart

Time	Systolic (Upper)	Diastolic (Lower)	Heart Rate

Medications

Three Goals for Today...

1. _______________________

2. _______________________

3. _______________________

Notes

What impacted your mood today?

What activities or people brought positivity to your day?

What thoughts or events made you feel anxious or upset today?

How did you cope with those feelings?

Did you practice self-care today? If not, what self-care activities can you plan for tomorrow?

Date: _________   Day   M   T   W   T   F   S   S

Hours of Sleep: _________

Mood (Morning)

😃 🙂 😐 🙁 😠

Evening (Morning)

😃 🙂 😐 🙁 😠

Water Intake	Energy Level

Did you feel any of the following today?

- [ ] Energized
- [ ] Happy
- [ ] Motivated
- [ ] Excited
- [ ] Sad
- [ ] Upset
- [ ] Lost
- [ ] Angry
- [ ] Optimistic
- [ ] Creative
- [ ] Joyful
- [ ] Productive
- [ ] Bored
- [ ] Annoyed
- [ ] Confused
- [ ] Hesitant

Food Intake

Breakfast	Lunch	Dinner	Snacks

Blood Pressure Chart

Time	Systolic (Upper)	Diastolic (Lower)	Heart Rate

Medications

Three Goals for Today...

1.

2.

3.

Notes

What impacted your mood today?

What activities or people brought positivity to your day?

What thoughts or events made you feel anxious or upset today?

How did you cope with those feelings?

Did you practice self-care today? If not, what self-care activities can you plan for tomorrow?

Date: __________   Day   M   T   W   T   F   S   S

Hours of Sleep: __________

Mood (Morning)

Evening (Morning)

Water Intake

Energy Level

Did you feel any of the following today?

- ☐ Energized
- ☐ Happy
- ☐ Motivated
- ☐ Excited
- ☐ Sad
- ☐ Upset
- ☐ Lost
- ☐ Angry
- ☐ Optimistic
- ☐ Creative
- ☐ Joyful
- ☐ Productive
- ☐ Bored
- ☐ Annoyed
- ☐ Confused
- ☐ Hesitant

Food Intake

Breakfast	Lunch	Dinner	Snacks

Blood Pressure Chart

Time	Systolic (Upper)	Diastolic (Lower)	Heart Rate

Medications

Three Goals for Today...   Notes

1. _______________

2. _______________

3. _______________

What impacted your mood today?

What activities or people brought positivity to your day?

What thoughts or events made you feel anxious or upset today?

How did you cope with those feelings?

Did you practice self-care today? If not, what self-care activities can you plan for tomorrow?

Date: __________ Day M T W T F S S

Hours of Sleep: __________

Mood (Morning)

Evening (Morning)

Water Intake

Energy Level

Did you feel any of the following today?

- [ ] Energized
- [ ] Happy
- [ ] Motivated
- [ ] Excited
- [ ] Sad
- [ ] Upset
- [ ] Lost
- [ ] Angry
- [ ] Optimistic
- [ ] Creative
- [ ] Joyful
- [ ] Productive
- [ ] Bored
- [ ] Annoyed
- [ ] Confused
- [ ] Hesitant

Food Intake

Breakfast	Lunch	Dinner	Snacks

Blood Pressure Chart

Time	Systolic (Upper)	Diastolic (Lower)	Heart Rate

Medications

Three Goals for Today...

Notes

1. __________

2. __________

3. __________

What impacted your mood today?

What activities or people brought positivity to your day?

What thoughts or events made you feel anxious or upset today?

How did you cope with those feelings?

Did you practice self-care today? If not, what self-care activities can you plan for tomorrow?

Date: _____________ Day   M   T   W   T   F   S   S

Hours of Sleep: _____________

Mood (Morning)

Water Intake

Energy Level

Evening (Morning)

Did you feel any of the following today?

- [ ] Energized
- [ ] Happy
- [ ] Motivated
- [ ] Excited
- [ ] Sad
- [ ] Upset
- [ ] Lost
- [ ] Angry
- [ ] Optimistic
- [ ] Creative
- [ ] Joyful
- [ ] Productive
- [ ] Bored
- [ ] Annoyed
- [ ] Confused
- [ ] Hesitant

Food Intake

Breakfast	Lunch	Dinner	Snacks

Blood Pressure Chart

Time	Systolic (Upper)	Diastolic (Lower)	Heart Rate

Medications

Three Goals for Today...

Notes

1.

2.

3.

What impacted your mood today?

What activities or people brought positivity to your day?

What thoughts or events made you feel anxious or upset today?

How did you cope with those feelings?

Did you practice self-care today? If not, what self-care activities can you plan for tomorrow?

Date: _____________   Day   M   T   W   T   F   S   S

Hours of Sleep: _____________

Mood (Morning)

Evening (Morning)

Water Intake	Energy Level

Did you feel any of the following today?

- ☐ Energized ☐ Happy   ☐ Motivated ☐ Excited
- ☐ Sad   ☐ Upset   ☐ Lost   ☐ Angry
- ☐ Optimistic ☐ Creative ☐ Joyful   ☐ Productive
- ☐ Bored   ☐ Annoyed   ☐ Confused   ☐ Hesitant

Food Intake

Breakfast	Lunch	Dinner	Snacks

Blood Pressure Chart

Time	Systolic (Upper)	Diastolic (Lower)	Heart Rate

Medications

Three Goals for Today...   Notes

1. _______________________

2. _______________________

3. _______________________

What impacted your mood today?

What activities or people brought positivity to your day?

What thoughts or events made you feel anxious or upset today?

How did you cope with those feelings?

Did you practice self-care today? If not, what self-care activities can you plan for tomorrow?

Date: _____________ Day   M   T   W   T   F   S   S

Hours of Sleep: _____________

Mood (Morning)

Evening (Morning)

| Water Intake | Energy Level |

Did you feel any of the following today?

☐ Energized	☐ Happy	☐ Motivated	☐ Excited
☐ Sad	☐ Upset	☐ Lost	☐ Angry
☐ Optimistic	☐ Creative	☐ Joyful	☐ Productive
☐ Bored	☐ Annoyed	☐ Confused	☐ Hesitant

Food Intake

Breakfast	Lunch	Dinner	Snacks

Blood Pressure Chart

Time	Systolic (Upper)	Diastolic (Lower)	Heart Rate

Medications

Three Goals for Today...

1. _____________________

2. _____________________

3. _____________________

Notes

What impacted your mood today?

What activities or people brought positivity to your day?

What thoughts or events made you feel anxious or upset today?

How did you cope with those feelings?

Did you practice self-care today? If not, what self-care activities can you plan for tomorrow?

Date: _______________   Day   M   T   W   T   F   S   S

Hours of Sleep: _______________

Mood (Morning)

Evening (Morning)

Water Intake	Energy Level

Did you feel any of the following today?

☐ Energized	☐ Happy	☐ Motivated	☐ Excited
☐ Sad	☐ Upset	☐ Lost	☐ Angry
☐ Optimistic	☐ Creative	☐ Joyful	☐ Productive
☐ Bored	☐ Annoyed	☐ Confused	☐ Hesitant

Food Intake

Breakfast	Lunch	Dinner	Snacks

Blood Pressure Chart

Time	Systolic (Upper)	Diastolic (Lower)	Heart Rate

Medications

Three Goals for Today...   Notes

1. _______________________________

2. _______________________________

3. _______________________________

What impacted your mood today?

What activities or people brought positivity to your day?

What thoughts or events made you feel anxious or upset today?

How did you cope with those feelings?

Did you practice self-care today? If not, what self-care activities can you plan for tomorrow?

Date: ___________ Day   M   T   W   T   F   S   S

Hours of Sleep: ___________

Mood (Morning)

Evening (Morning)

Water Intake

Energy Level

Did you feel any of the following today?

- ☐ Energized
- ☐ Happy
- ☐ Motivated
- ☐ Excited
- ☐ Sad
- ☐ Upset
- ☐ Lost
- ☐ Angry
- ☐ Optimistic
- ☐ Creative
- ☐ Joyful
- ☐ Productive
- ☐ Bored
- ☐ Annoyed
- ☐ Confused
- ☐ Hesitant

Food Intake

Breakfast	Lunch	Dinner	Snacks

Blood Pressure Chart

Time	Systolic (Upper)	Diastolic (Lower)	Heart Rate

Medications

Three Goals for Today...

Notes

1. _______________________________

2. _______________________________

3. _______________________________

What impacted your mood today?

What activities or people brought positivity to your day?

What thoughts or events made you feel anxious or upset today?

How did you cope with those feelings?

Did you practice self-care today? If not, what self-care activities can you plan for tomorrow?

Date: __________   Day   M   T   W   T   F   S   S

Hours of Sleep: __________

Mood (Morning)

😃   🙂   😐   🙁   😠

Evening (Morning)

😃   🙂   😐   🙁   😠

	Water Intake	Energy Level

Did you feel any of the following today?

- ☐ Energized
- ☐ Happy
- ☐ Motivated
- ☐ Excited
- ☐ Sad
- ☐ Upset
- ☐ Lost
- ☐ Angry
- ☐ Optimistic
- ☐ Creative
- ☐ Joyful
- ☐ Productive
- ☐ Bored
- ☐ Annoyed
- ☐ Confused
- ☐ Hesitant

Food Intake

Breakfast	Lunch	Dinner	Snacks

Blood Pressure Chart

Time	Systolic (Upper)	Diastolic (Lower)	Heart Rate

Medications

Three Goals for Today...

1. _______________________________

2. _______________________________

3. _______________________________

Notes

What impacted your mood today?

What activities or people brought positivity to your day?

What thoughts or events made you feel anxious or upset today?

How did you cope with those feelings?

Did you practice self-care today? If not, what self-care activities can you plan for tomorrow?

Date: ___________   Day   M   T   W   T   F   S   S

Hours of Sleep: ___________

Mood (Morning)

Evening (Morning)

Water Intake

Energy Level

Did you feel any of the following today?

☐ Energized	☐ Happy	☐ Motivated	☐ Excited
☐ Sad	☐ Upset	☐ Lost	☐ Angry
☐ Optimistic	☐ Creative	☐ Joyful	☐ Productive
☐ Bored	☐ Annoyed	☐ Confused	☐ Hesitant

Food Intake

Breakfast	Lunch	Dinner	Snacks

Blood Pressure Chart

Time	Systolic (Upper)	Diastolic (Lower)	Heart Rate

Medications

Three Goals for Today...

1.
2.
3.

Notes

What impacted your mood today?

What activities or people brought positivity to your day?

What thoughts or events made you feel anxious or upset today?

How did you cope with those feelings?

Did you practice self-care today? If not, what self-care activities can you plan for tomorrow?

Date: _____________ Day   M   T   W   T   F   S   S

Hours of Sleep: _____________

Mood (Morning)

Evening (Morning)

Water Intake	Energy Level

Did you feel any of the following today?

- [ ] Energized
- [ ] Happy
- [ ] Motivated
- [ ] Excited
- [ ] Sad
- [ ] Upset
- [ ] Lost
- [ ] Angry
- [ ] Optimistic
- [ ] Creative
- [ ] Joyful
- [ ] Productive
- [ ] Bored
- [ ] Annoyed
- [ ] Confused
- [ ] Hesitant

Food Intake

Breakfast	Lunch	Dinner	Snacks

Blood Pressure Chart

Time	Systolic (Upper)	Diastolic (Lower)	Heart Rate

Medications

Three Goals for Today...

1. _______________________________
2. _______________________________
3. _______________________________

Notes

What impacted your mood today?

What activities or people brought positivity to your day?

What thoughts or events made you feel anxious or upset today?

How did you cope with those feelings?

Did you practice self-care today? If not, what self-care activities can you plan for tomorrow?

Date: _____________ Day M T W T F S S

Hours of Sleep: _____________

Mood (Morning)

😄 🙂 😐 🙁 😠

Evening (Morning)

😄 🙂 😐 🙁 😠

Water Intake	Energy Level

Did you feel any of the following today?

☐ Energized	☐ Happy	☐ Motivated	☐ Excited
☐ Sad	☐ Upset	☐ Lost	☐ Angry
☐ Optimistic	☐ Creative	☐ Joyful	☐ Productive
☐ Bored	☐ Annoyed	☐ Confused	☐ Hesitant

Food Intake

Breakfast	Lunch	Dinner	Snacks

Blood Pressure Chart

Time	Systolic (Upper)	Diastolic (Lower)	Heart Rate

Medications

Three Goals for Today...

1. _______________________

2. _______________________

3. _______________________

Notes

What impacted your mood today?

What activities or people brought positivity to your day?

What thoughts or events made you feel anxious or upset today?

How did you cope with those feelings?

Did you practice self-care today? If not, what self-care activities can you plan for tomorrow?

Date: __________ Day M T W T F S S

Hours of Sleep: __________

Mood (Morning)

Evening (Morning)

| Water Intake | Energy Level |

Did you feel any of the following today?

- ☐ Energized
- ☐ Happy
- ☐ Motivated
- ☐ Excited
- ☐ Sad
- ☐ Upset
- ☐ Lost
- ☐ Angry
- ☐ Optimistic
- ☐ Creative
- ☐ Joyful
- ☐ Productive
- ☐ Bored
- ☐ Annoyed
- ☐ Confused
- ☐ Hesitant

Food Intake

Breakfast	Lunch	Dinner	Snacks

Blood Pressure Chart

Time	Systolic (Upper)	Diastolic (Lower)	Heart Rate

Medications

Three Goals for Today...   Notes

1. __________________________________

2. __________________________________

3. __________________________________

What impacted your mood today?

What activities or people brought positivity to your day?

What thoughts or events made you feel anxious or upset today?

How did you cope with those feelings?

Did you practice self-care today? If not, what self-care activities can you plan for tomorrow?

Date: _______________   Day   M   T   W   T   F   S   S

Hours of Sleep: _______________

Mood (Morning)

Evening (Morning)

Water Intake	Energy Level

Did you feel any of the following today?

- [ ] Energized
- [ ] Happy
- [ ] Motivated
- [ ] Excited
- [ ] Sad
- [ ] Upset
- [ ] Lost
- [ ] Angry
- [ ] Optimistic
- [ ] Creative
- [ ] Joyful
- [ ] Productive
- [ ] Bored
- [ ] Annoyed
- [ ] Confused
- [ ] Hesitant

Food Intake

Breakfast	Lunch	Dinner	Snacks

Blood Pressure Chart

Time	Systolic (Upper)	Diastolic (Lower)	Heart Rate

Medications

Three Goals for Today...

1. ______________________________

2. ______________________________

3. ______________________________

Notes

What impacted your mood today?

What activities or people brought positivity to your day?

What thoughts or events made you feel anxious or upset today?

How did you cope with those feelings?

Did you practice self-care today? If not, what self-care activities can you plan for tomorrow?

Date: _______________   Day   M   T   W   T   F   S   S

Hours of Sleep: _______________

Mood (Morning)

Evening (Morning)

Water Intake	Energy Level

Did you feel any of the following today?

- ☐ Energized
- ☐ Happy
- ☐ Motivated
- ☐ Excited
- ☐ Sad
- ☐ Upset
- ☐ Lost
- ☐ Angry
- ☐ Optimistic
- ☐ Creative
- ☐ Joyful
- ☐ Productive
- ☐ Bored
- ☐ Annoyed
- ☐ Confused
- ☐ Hesitant

Food Intake

Breakfast	Lunch	Dinner	Snacks

Blood Pressure Chart

Time	Systolic (Upper)	Diastolic (Lower)	Heart Rate

Medications

Three Goals for Today...

1. _______________________________________

2. _______________________________________

3. _______________________________________

Notes

What impacted your mood today?

What activities or people brought positivity to your day?

What thoughts or events made you feel anxious or upset today?

How did you cope with those feelings?

Did you practice self-care today? If not, what self-care activities can you plan for tomorrow?

Date: _________   Day   M   T   W   T   F   S   S

Hours of Sleep: _________

Mood (Morning)

Evening (Morning)

Water Intake

Energy Level

Did you feel any of the following today?

- [ ] Energized
- [ ] Happy
- [ ] Motivated
- [ ] Excited
- [ ] Sad
- [ ] Upset
- [ ] Lost
- [ ] Angry
- [ ] Optimistic
- [ ] Creative
- [ ] Joyful
- [ ] Productive
- [ ] Bored
- [ ] Annoyed
- [ ] Confused
- [ ] Hesitant

Food Intake

Breakfast	Lunch	Dinner	Snacks

Blood Pressure Chart

Time	Systolic (Upper)	Diastolic (Lower)	Heart Rate

Medications

Three Goals for Today...

1. ___________________________

2. ___________________________

3. ___________________________

Notes

What impacted your mood today?

What activities or people brought positivity to your day?

What thoughts or events made you feel anxious or upset today?

How did you cope with those feelings?

Did you practice self-care today? If not, what self-care activities can you plan for tomorrow?

Date: _______________   Day   M   T   W   T   F   S   S

Hours of Sleep: _______________

Did you feel any of the following today?

- [ ] Energized
- [ ] Happy
- [ ] Motivated
- [ ] Excited
- [ ] Sad
- [ ] Upset
- [ ] Lost
- [ ] Angry
- [ ] Optimistic
- [ ] Creative
- [ ] Joyful
- [ ] Productive
- [ ] Bored
- [ ] Annoyed
- [ ] Confused
- [ ] Hesitant

Food Intake

Breakfast	Lunch	Dinner	Snacks

Blood Pressure Chart

Time	Systolic (Upper)	Diastolic (Lower)	Heart Rate

Medications

Three Goals for Today...

1. ______________________________

2. ______________________________

3. ______________________________

Notes

What impacted your mood today?

What activities or people brought positivity to your day?

What thoughts or events made you feel anxious or upset today?

How did you cope with those feelings?

Did you practice self-care today? If not, what self-care activities can you plan for tomorrow?

Date: _____________   Day   M   T   W   T   F   S   S

Hours of Sleep: _____________

Mood (Morning)

Evening (Morning)

Water Intake | Energy Level

Did you feel any of the following today?

- [ ] Energized
- [ ] Happy
- [ ] Motivated
- [ ] Excited
- [ ] Sad
- [ ] Upset
- [ ] Lost
- [ ] Angry
- [ ] Optimistic
- [ ] Creative
- [ ] Joyful
- [ ] Productive
- [ ] Bored
- [ ] Annoyed
- [ ] Confused
- [ ] Hesitant

Food Intake

Breakfast	Lunch	Dinner	Snacks

Blood Pressure Chart

Time	Systolic (Upper)	Diastolic (Lower)	Heart Rate

Medications

Three Goals for Today...   Notes

1.

2.

3.

What impacted your mood today?

What activities or people brought positivity to your day?

What thoughts or events made you feel anxious or upset today?

How did you cope with those feelings?

Did you practice self-care today? If not, what self-care activities can you plan for tomorrow?

Date: _______________   Day   M   T   W   T   F   S   S

Hours of Sleep: _______________

Mood (Morning)

Evening (Morning)

Water Intake

Energy Level

Did you feel any of the following today?

- [ ] Energized
- [ ] Happy
- [ ] Motivated
- [ ] Excited
- [ ] Sad
- [ ] Upset
- [ ] Lost
- [ ] Angry
- [ ] Optimistic
- [ ] Creative
- [ ] Joyful
- [ ] Productive
- [ ] Bored
- [ ] Annoyed
- [ ] Confused
- [ ] Hesitant

Food Intake

Breakfast	Lunch	Dinner	Snacks

Blood Pressure Chart

Time	Systolic (Upper)	Diastolic (Lower)	Heart Rate

Medications

Three Goals for Today...

Notes

1. _______________

2. _______________

3. _______________

What impacted your mood today?

What activities or people brought positivity to your day?

What thoughts or events made you feel anxious or upset today?

How did you cope with those feelings?

Did you practice self-care today? If not, what self-care activities can you plan for tomorrow?

Date: _____________ Day   M   T   W   T   F   S   S

Hours of Sleep: _____________

Mood (Morning)

Evening (Morning)

Water Intake

Energy Level

Did you feel any of the following today?

- [ ] Energized
- [ ] Happy
- [ ] Motivated
- [ ] Excited
- [ ] Sad
- [ ] Upset
- [ ] Lost
- [ ] Angry
- [ ] Optimistic
- [ ] Creative
- [ ] Joyful
- [ ] Productive
- [ ] Bored
- [ ] Annoyed
- [ ] Confused
- [ ] Hesitant

Food Intake

Breakfast	Lunch	Dinner	Snacks

Blood Pressure Chart

Time	Systolic (Upper)	Diastolic (Lower)	Heart Rate

Medications

Three Goals for Today...

Notes

1. _______________________________

2. _______________________________

3. _______________________________

What impacted your mood today?

What activities or people brought positivity to your day?

What thoughts or events made you feel anxious or upset today?

How did you cope with those feelings?

Did you practice self-care today? If not, what self-care activities can you plan for tomorrow?

Date: __________   Day   M   T   W   T   F   S   S

Hours of Sleep: __________

Mood (Morning)

Evening (Morning)

| Water Intake | Energy Level |

Did you feel any of the following today?

- [ ] Energized
- [ ] Happy
- [ ] Motivated
- [ ] Excited
- [ ] Sad
- [ ] Upset
- [ ] Lost
- [ ] Angry
- [ ] Optimistic
- [ ] Creative
- [ ] Joyful
- [ ] Productive
- [ ] Bored
- [ ] Annoyed
- [ ] Confused
- [ ] Hesitant

Food Intake

Breakfast	Lunch	Dinner	Snacks

Blood Pressure Chart

Time	Systolic (Upper)	Diastolic (Lower)	Heart Rate

Medications

Three Goals for Today...

Notes

1.

2.

3.

What impacted your mood today?

What activities or people brought positivity to your day?

What thoughts or events made you feel anxious or upset today?

How did you cope with those feelings?

Did you practice self-care today? If not, what self-care activities can you plan for tomorrow?

Date: __________   Day   M   T   W   T   F   S   S

Hours of Sleep: __________

Mood (Morning)

Evening (Morning)

Water Intake	Energy Level

Did you feel any of the following today?

- ☐ Energized
- ☐ Happy
- ☐ Motivated
- ☐ Excited
- ☐ Sad
- ☐ Upset
- ☐ Lost
- ☐ Angry
- ☐ Optimistic
- ☐ Creative
- ☐ Joyful
- ☐ Productive
- ☐ Bored
- ☐ Annoyed
- ☐ Confused
- ☐ Hesitant

Food Intake

Breakfast	Lunch	Dinner	Snacks

Blood Pressure Chart

Time	Systolic (Upper)	Diastolic (Lower)	Heart Rate

Medications

Three Goals for Today...

1. __________

2. __________

3. __________

Notes

What impacted your mood today?

What activities or people brought positivity to your day?

What thoughts or events made you feel anxious or upset today?

How did you cope with those feelings?

Did you practice self-care today? If not, what self-care activities can you plan for tomorrow?

Date: _____________ Day   M   T   W   T   F   S   S

Hours of Sleep: _______________

Mood (Morning)

Evening (Morning)

Water Intake	Energy Level

Did you feel any of the following today?

- [ ] Energized
- [ ] Happy
- [ ] Motivated
- [ ] Excited
- [ ] Sad
- [ ] Upset
- [ ] Lost
- [ ] Angry
- [ ] Optimistic
- [ ] Creative
- [ ] Joyful
- [ ] Productive
- [ ] Bored
- [ ] Annoyed
- [ ] Confused
- [ ] Hesitant

Food Intake

Breakfast	Lunch	Dinner	Snacks

Blood Pressure Chart

Time	Systolic (Upper)	Diastolic (Lower)	Heart Rate

Medications

Three Goals for Today...

1. _______________________________

2. _______________________________

3. _______________________________

Notes

What impacted your mood today?

What activities or people brought positivity to your day?

What thoughts or events made you feel anxious or upset today?

How did you cope with those feelings?

Did you practice self-care today? If not, what self-care activities can you plan for tomorrow?

Date: __________   Day   M   T   W   T   F   S   S

Hours of Sleep: __________

Mood (Morning)

Evening (Morning)

Water Intake

Energy Level

Did you feel any of the following today?

- [ ] Energized
- [ ] Happy
- [ ] Motivated
- [ ] Excited
- [ ] Sad
- [ ] Upset
- [ ] Lost
- [ ] Angry
- [ ] Optimistic
- [ ] Creative
- [ ] Joyful
- [ ] Productive
- [ ] Bored
- [ ] Annoyed
- [ ] Confused
- [ ] Hesitant

Food Intake

Breakfast	Lunch	Dinner	Snacks

Blood Pressure Chart

Time	Systolic (Upper)	Diastolic (Lower)	Heart Rate

Medications

Three Goals for Today...

Notes

1. ___________________________

2. ___________________________

3. ___________________________

What impacted your mood today?

What activities or people brought positivity to your day?

What thoughts or events made you feel anxious or upset today?

How did you cope with those feelings?

Did you practice self-care today? If not, what self-care activities can you plan for tomorrow?

Date: __________   Day   M   T   W   T   F   S   S

Hours of Sleep: __________

| Water Intake | Energy Level |

Mood (Morning)

Evening (Morning)

Did you feel any of the following today?

- [ ] Energized
- [ ] Happy
- [ ] Motivated
- [ ] Excited
- [ ] Sad
- [ ] Upset
- [ ] Lost
- [ ] Angry
- [ ] Optimistic
- [ ] Creative
- [ ] Joyful
- [ ] Productive
- [ ] Bored
- [ ] Annoyed
- [ ] Confused
- [ ] Hesitant

Food Intake

Breakfast	Lunch	Dinner	Snacks

Blood Pressure Chart

Time	Systolic (Upper)	Diastolic (Lower)	Heart Rate

Medications

Three Goals for Today...   Notes

1. ________________

2. ________________

3. ________________

What impacted your mood today?

What activities or people brought positivity to your day?

What thoughts or events made you feel anxious or upset today?

How did you cope with those feelings?

Did you practice self-care today? If not, what self-care activities can you plan for tomorrow?

Date: _____________   Day   M   T   W   T   F   S   S

Hours of Sleep: _____________

| Water Intake | Energy Level |

Mood (Morning)

☺ ☺ ☺ ☹ 😠

Evening (Morning)

☺ ☺ ☺ ☹ 😠

Did you feel any of the following today?

- [ ] Energized
- [ ] Happy
- [ ] Motivated
- [ ] Excited
- [ ] Sad
- [ ] Upset
- [ ] Lost
- [ ] Angry
- [ ] Optimistic
- [ ] Creative
- [ ] Joyful
- [ ] Productive
- [ ] Bored
- [ ] Annoyed
- [ ] Confused
- [ ] Hesitant

Food Intake

Breakfast	Lunch	Dinner	Snacks

Blood Pressure Chart

Time	Systolic (Upper)	Diastolic (Lower)	Heart Rate

Medications

Three Goals for Today...

1. _______________________

2. _______________________

3. _______________________

Notes

What impacted your mood today?

What activities or people brought positivity to your day?

What thoughts or events made you feel anxious or upset today?

How did you cope with those feelings?

Did you practice self-care today? If not, what self-care activities can you plan for tomorrow?

Date: _______________   Day   M   T   W   T   F   S   S

Hours of Sleep: _______________

Mood (Morning)

Evening (Morning)

Water Intake	Energy Level

Did you feel any of the following today?

☐ Energized	☐ Happy	☐ Motivated	☐ Excited
☐ Sad	☐ Upset	☐ Lost	☐ Angry
☐ Optimistic	☐ Creative	☐ Joyful	☐ Productive
☐ Bored	☐ Annoyed	☐ Confused	☐ Hesitant

Food Intake

Breakfast	Lunch	Dinner	Snacks

Blood Pressure Chart

Time	Systolic (Upper)	Diastolic (Lower)	Heart Rate

Medications

Three Goals for Today...

Notes

1. _______________

2. _______________

3. _______________

What impacted your mood today?

What activities or people brought positivity to your day?

What thoughts or events made you feel anxious or upset today?

How did you cope with those feelings?

Did you practice self-care today? If not, what self-care activities can you plan for tomorrow?

Date: _____________   Day   M   T   W   T   F   S   S

Hours of Sleep: _____________

Mood (Morning)

☺ 🙂 😐 🙁 😠

Evening (Morning)

☺ 🙂 😐 🙁 😠

Water Intake	Energy Level

Did you feel any of the following today?

- ☐ Energized
- ☐ Happy
- ☐ Motivated
- ☐ Excited
- ☐ Sad
- ☐ Upset
- ☐ Lost
- ☐ Angry
- ☐ Optimistic
- ☐ Creative
- ☐ Joyful
- ☐ Productive
- ☐ Bored
- ☐ Annoyed
- ☐ Confused
- ☐ Hesitant

Food Intake

Breakfast	Lunch	Dinner	Snacks

Blood Pressure Chart

Time	Systolic (Upper)	Diastolic (Lower)	Heart Rate

Medications

Three Goals for Today...

1.
2.
3.

Notes

What impacted your mood today?

What activities or people brought positivity to your day?

What thoughts or events made you feel anxious or upset today?

How did you cope with those feelings?

Did you practice self-care today? If not, what self-care activities can you plan for tomorrow?

Date: __________   Day   M   T   W   T   F   S   S

Hours of Sleep: __________

Water Intake	Energy Level

Mood (Morning)

😄 🙂 😐 🙁 😠

Evening (Morning)

😄 🙂 😐 🙁 😠

Did you feel any of the following today?

☐ Energized	☐ Happy	☐ Motivated	☐ Excited
☐ Sad	☐ Upset	☐ Lost	☐ Angry
☐ Optimistic	☐ Creative	☐ Joyful	☐ Productive
☐ Bored	☐ Annoyed	☐ Confused	☐ Hesitant

Food Intake

Breakfast	Lunch	Dinner	Snacks

Blood Pressure Chart

Time	Systolic (Upper)	Diastolic (Lower)	Heart Rate

Medications

Three Goals for Today...

1.

2.

3.

Notes

What impacted your mood today?

What activities or people brought positivity to your day?

What thoughts or events made you feel anxious or upset today?

How did you cope with those feelings?

Did you practice self-care today? If not, what self-care activities can you plan for tomorrow?

Date: _____________   Day   M   T   W   T   F   S   S

Hours of Sleep: _____________

Water Intake	Energy Level

Mood (Morning)

Evening (Morning)

Did you feel any of the following today?

- ☐ Energized
- ☐ Happy
- ☐ Motivated
- ☐ Excited
- ☐ Sad
- ☐ Upset
- ☐ Lost
- ☐ Angry
- ☐ Optimistic
- ☐ Creative
- ☐ Joyful
- ☐ Productive
- ☐ Bored
- ☐ Annoyed
- ☐ Confused
- ☐ Hesitant

Food Intake

Breakfast	Lunch	Dinner	Snacks

Blood Pressure Chart

Time	Systolic (Upper)	Diastolic (Lower)	Heart Rate

Medications

Three Goals for Today...   Notes

1. _______________________

2. _______________________

3. _______________________

What impacted your mood today?

What activities or people brought positivity to your day?

What thoughts or events made you feel anxious or upset today?

How did you cope with those feelings?

Did you practice self-care today? If not, what self-care activities can you plan for tomorrow?

Date: _________   Day   M   T   W   T   F   S   S

Hours of Sleep: _________

Mood (Morning)

Water Intake

Energy Level

Evening (Morning)

Did you feel any of the following today?

- [ ] Energized
- [ ] Happy
- [ ] Motivated
- [ ] Excited
- [ ] Sad
- [ ] Upset
- [ ] Lost
- [ ] Angry
- [ ] Optimistic
- [ ] Creative
- [ ] Joyful
- [ ] Productive
- [ ] Bored
- [ ] Annoyed
- [ ] Confused
- [ ] Hesitant

Food Intake

Breakfast	Lunch	Dinner	Snacks

Blood Pressure Chart

Time	Systolic (Upper)	Diastolic (Lower)	Heart Rate

Medications

Three Goals for Today...

Notes

1.
2.
3.

What impacted your mood today?

What activities or people brought positivity to your day?

What thoughts or events made you feel anxious or upset today?

How did you cope with those feelings?

Did you practice self-care today? If not, what self-care activities can you plan for tomorrow?

Date: _______________ Day   M   T   W   T   F   S   S

Hours of Sleep: _______________

| Water Intake | Energy Level |

Mood (Morning)

Evening (Morning)

Did you feel any of the following today?

- [ ] Energized
- [ ] Happy
- [ ] Motivated
- [ ] Excited
- [ ] Sad
- [ ] Upset
- [ ] Lost
- [ ] Angry
- [ ] Optimistic
- [ ] Creative
- [ ] Joyful
- [ ] Productive
- [ ] Bored
- [ ] Annoyed
- [ ] Confused
- [ ] Hesitant

Food Intake

Breakfast	Lunch	Dinner	Snacks

Blood Pressure Chart

Time	Systolic (Upper)	Diastolic (Lower)	Heart Rate

Medications

Three Goals for Today...

Notes

1.

2.

3.

What impacted your mood today?

What activities or people brought positivity to your day?

What thoughts or events made you feel anxious or upset today?

How did you cope with those feelings?

Did you practice self-care today? If not, what self-care activities can you plan for tomorrow?

Date: _____________   Day   M   T   W   T   F   S   S

Hours of Sleep: _____________

Mood (Morning)

Evening (Morning)

Water Intake	Energy Level

Did you feel any of the following today?

- ☐ Energized
- ☐ Happy
- ☐ Motivated
- ☐ Excited
- ☐ Sad
- ☐ Upset
- ☐ Lost
- ☐ Angry
- ☐ Optimistic
- ☐ Creative
- ☐ Joyful
- ☐ Productive
- ☐ Bored
- ☐ Annoyed
- ☐ Confused
- ☐ Hesitant

Food Intake

Breakfast	Lunch	Dinner	Snacks

Blood Pressure Chart

Time	Systolic (Upper)	Diastolic (Lower)	Heart Rate

Medications

Three Goals for Today...

1. _______________________

2. _______________________

3. _______________________

Notes

What impacted your mood today?

What activities or people brought positivity to your day?

What thoughts or events made you feel anxious or upset today?

How did you cope with those feelings?

Did you practice self-care today? If not, what self-care activities can you plan for tomorrow?

Date: _____________   Day   M   T   W   T   F   S   S

Hours of Sleep: _____________

Mood (Morning)

Evening (Morning)

| Water Intake | Energy Level |

Did you feel any of the following today?

☐ Energized	☐ Happy	☐ Motivated	☐ Excited
☐ Sad	☐ Upset	☐ Lost	☐ Angry
☐ Optimistic	☐ Creative	☐ Joyful	☐ Productive
☐ Bored	☐ Annoyed	☐ Confused	☐ Hesitant

Food Intake

Breakfast	Lunch	Dinner	Snacks

Blood Pressure Chart

Time	Systolic (Upper)	Diastolic (Lower)	Heart Rate

Medications

Three Goals for Today...

Notes

1.

2.

3.

What impacted your mood today?

What activities or people brought positivity to your day?

What thoughts or events made you feel anxious or upset today?

How did you cope with those feelings?

Did you practice self-care today? If not, what self-care activities can you plan for tomorrow?

Date: _________________   Day   M   T   W   T   F   S   S

Hours of Sleep: _________________

Mood (Morning)

Evening (Morning)

| Water Intake | Energy Level |

Did you feel any of the following today?

☐ Energized	☐ Happy	☐ Motivated	☐ Excited
☐ Sad	☐ Upset	☐ Lost	☐ Angry
☐ Optimistic	☐ Creative	☐ Joyful	☐ Productive
☐ Bored	☐ Annoyed	☐ Confused	☐ Hesitant

Food Intake

Breakfast	Lunch	Dinner	Snacks

Blood Pressure Chart

Time	Systolic (Upper)	Diastolic (Lower)	Heart Rate

Medications

Three Goals for Today...   Notes

1. _______________________

2. _______________________

3. _______________________

What impacted your mood today?

What activities or people brought positivity to your day?

What thoughts or events made you feel anxious or upset today?

How did you cope with those feelings?

Did you practice self-care today? If not, what self-care activities can you plan for tomorrow?

Date: _____________   Day   M   T   W   T   F   S   S

Hours of Sleep: _____________

Mood (Morning)

Evening (Morning)

Water Intake

Energy Level

Did you feel any of the following today?

☐ Energized	☐ Happy	☐ Motivated	☐ Excited
☐ Sad	☐ Upset	☐ Lost	☐ Angry
☐ Optimistic	☐ Creative	☐ Joyful	☐ Productive
☐ Bored	☐ Annoyed	☐ Confused	☐ Hesitant

Food Intake

Breakfast	Lunch	Dinner	Snacks

Blood Pressure Chart

Time	Systolic (Upper)	Diastolic (Lower)	Heart Rate

Medications

Three Goals for Today...

Notes

1.

2.

3.

What impacted your mood today?

What activities or people brought positivity to your day?

What thoughts or events made you feel anxious or upset today?

How did you cope with those feelings?

Did you practice self-care today? If not, what self-care activities can you plan for tomorrow?

Date: __________ Day M T W T F S S

Hours of Sleep: __________

Mood (Morning)

Evening (Morning)

| Water Intake | Energy Level |

Did you feel any of the following today?

- [ ] Energized
- [ ] Happy
- [ ] Motivated
- [ ] Excited
- [ ] Sad
- [ ] Upset
- [ ] Lost
- [ ] Angry
- [ ] Optimistic
- [ ] Creative
- [ ] Joyful
- [ ] Productive
- [ ] Bored
- [ ] Annoyed
- [ ] Confused
- [ ] Hesitant

Food Intake

Breakfast	Lunch	Dinner	Snacks

Blood Pressure Chart

Time	Systolic (Upper)	Diastolic (Lower)	Heart Rate

Medications

Three Goals for Today...

Notes

1.

2.

3.

What impacted your mood today?

What activities or people brought positivity to your day?

What thoughts or events made you feel anxious or upset today?

How did you cope with those feelings?

Did you practice self-care today? If not, what self-care activities can you plan for tomorrow?

Date: _____________ Day M T W T F S S

Hours of Sleep: _____________

Water Intake	Energy Level

Mood (Morning)

😀 🙂 😐 🙁 😠

Evening (Morning)

😀 🙂 😐 🙁 😠

Did you feel any of the following today?

- ☐ Energized
- ☐ Happy
- ☐ Motivated
- ☐ Excited
- ☐ Sad
- ☐ Upset
- ☐ Lost
- ☐ Angry
- ☐ Optimistic
- ☐ Creative
- ☐ Joyful
- ☐ Productive
- ☐ Bored
- ☐ Annoyed
- ☐ Confused
- ☐ Hesitant

Food Intake

Breakfast	Lunch	Dinner	Snacks

Blood Pressure Chart

Time	Systolic (Upper)	Diastolic (Lower)	Heart Rate

Medications

Three Goals for Today...

1.
2.
3.

Notes

What impacted your mood today?

What activities or people brought positivity to your day?

What thoughts or events made you feel anxious or upset today?

How did you cope with those feelings?

Did you practice self-care today? If not, what self-care activities can you plan for tomorrow?

Date: _____________   Day   M   T   W   T   F   S   S

Hours of Sleep: _____________

Mood (Morning)

Evening (Morning)

Water Intake	Energy Level

Did you feel any of the following today?

- [ ] Energized
- [ ] Happy
- [ ] Motivated
- [ ] Excited
- [ ] Sad
- [ ] Upset
- [ ] Lost
- [ ] Angry
- [ ] Optimistic
- [ ] Creative
- [ ] Joyful
- [ ] Productive
- [ ] Bored
- [ ] Annoyed
- [ ] Confused
- [ ] Hesitant

Food Intake

Breakfast	Lunch	Dinner	Snacks

Blood Pressure Chart

Time	Systolic (Upper)	Diastolic (Lower)	Heart Rate

Medications

Three Goals for Today...   Notes

1. _______________________

2. _______________________

3. _______________________

What impacted your mood today?

What activities or people brought positivity to your day?

What thoughts or events made you feel anxious or upset today?

How did you cope with those feelings?

Did you practice self-care today? If not, what self-care activities can you plan for tomorrow?

Date: __________ Day M T W T F S S

Hours of Sleep: __________

Mood (Morning)

Evening (Morning)

Water Intake

Energy Level

Did you feel any of the following today?

☐ Energized	☐ Happy	☐ Motivated	☐ Excited
☐ Sad	☐ Upset	☐ Lost	☐ Angry
☐ Optimistic	☐ Creative	☐ Joyful	☐ Productive
☐ Bored	☐ Annoyed	☐ Confused	☐ Hesitant

Food Intake

Breakfast	Lunch	Dinner	Snacks

Blood Pressure Chart

Time	Systolic (Upper)	Diastolic (Lower)	Heart Rate

Medications

Three Goals for Today...

1.

2.

3.

Notes

What impacted your mood today?

What activities or people brought positivity to your day?

What thoughts or events made you feel anxious or upset today?

How did you cope with those feelings?

Did you practice self-care today? If not, what self-care activities can you plan for tomorrow?

Date: _____________   Day   M   T   W   T   F   S   S

Hours of Sleep: _____________

Mood (Morning)

Evening (Morning)

| Water Intake | Energy Level |

Did you feel any of the following today?

- [ ] Energized
- [ ] Happy
- [ ] Motivated
- [ ] Excited
- [ ] Sad
- [ ] Upset
- [ ] Lost
- [ ] Angry
- [ ] Optimistic
- [ ] Creative
- [ ] Joyful
- [ ] Productive
- [ ] Bored
- [ ] Annoyed
- [ ] Confused
- [ ] Hesitant

Food Intake

Breakfast	Lunch	Dinner	Snacks

Blood Pressure Chart

Time	Systolic (Upper)	Diastolic (Lower)	Heart Rate

Medications

Three Goals for Today...

Notes

1.

2.

3.

What impacted your mood today?

What activities or people brought positivity to your day?

What thoughts or events made you feel anxious or upset today?

How did you cope with those feelings?

Did you practice self-care today? If not, what self-care activities can you plan for tomorrow?

Date: _____________   Day   M   T   W   T   F   S   S

Hours of Sleep: _____________

Mood (Morning)

Evening (Morning)

Water Intake	Energy Level

Did you feel any of the following today?

☐ Energized	☐ Happy	☐ Motivated	☐ Excited
☐ Sad	☐ Upset	☐ Lost	☐ Angry
☐ Optimistic	☐ Creative	☐ Joyful	☐ Productive
☐ Bored	☐ Annoyed	☐ Confused	☐ Hesitant

Food Intake

Breakfast	Lunch	Dinner	Snacks

Blood Pressure Chart

Time	Systolic (Upper)	Diastolic (Lower)	Heart Rate

Medications

Three Goals for Today...

1.

2.

3.

Notes

What impacted your mood today?

What activities or people brought positivity to your day?

What thoughts or events made you feel anxious or upset today?

How did you cope with those feelings?

Did you practice self-care today? If not, what self-care activities can you plan for tomorrow?

Date: _____________ Day M   T   W   T   F   S   S

Hours of Sleep: _____________

Water Intake	Energy Level

Mood (Morning)

Evening (Morning)

Did you feel any of the following today?

- [ ] Energized
- [ ] Happy
- [ ] Motivated
- [ ] Excited
- [ ] Sad
- [ ] Upset
- [ ] Lost
- [ ] Angry
- [ ] Optimistic
- [ ] Creative
- [ ] Joyful
- [ ] Productive
- [ ] Bored
- [ ] Annoyed
- [ ] Confused
- [ ] Hesitant

Food Intake

Breakfast	Lunch	Dinner	Snacks

Blood Pressure Chart

Time	Systolic (Upper)	Diastolic (Lower)	Heart Rate

Medications

Three Goals for Today...

1. _______________________

2. _______________________

3. _______________________

Notes

What impacted your mood today?

What activities or people brought positivity to your day?

What thoughts or events made you feel anxious or upset today?

How did you cope with those feelings?

Did you practice self-care today? If not, what self-care activities can you plan for tomorrow?

Date: __________   Day   M   T   W   T   F   S   S

Hours of Sleep: __________

Mood (Morning)

😁   🙂   😐   🙁   😠

Evening (Morning)

😁   🙂   😐   🙁   😠

Water Intake

Energy Level

Did you feel any of the following today?

- ☐ Energized
- ☐ Happy
- ☐ Motivated
- ☐ Excited
- ☐ Sad
- ☐ Upset
- ☐ Lost
- ☐ Angry
- ☐ Optimistic
- ☐ Creative
- ☐ Joyful
- ☐ Productive
- ☐ Bored
- ☐ Annoyed
- ☐ Confused
- ☐ Hesitant

Food Intake

Breakfast	Lunch	Dinner	Snacks

Blood Pressure Chart

Time	Systolic (Upper)	Diastolic (Lower)	Heart Rate

Medications

Three Goals for Today...

Notes

1. ______________________

2. ______________________

3. ______________________

What impacted your mood today?

What activities or people brought positivity to your day?

What thoughts or events made you feel anxious or upset today?

How did you cope with those feelings?

Did you practice self-care today? If not, what self-care activities can you plan for tomorrow?

Date: _____________ Day M T W T F S S

Hours of Sleep: _____________

Mood (Morning)

Evening (Morning)

Water Intake

Energy Level

Did you feel any of the following today?

- [ ] Energized
- [ ] Happy
- [ ] Motivated
- [ ] Excited
- [ ] Sad
- [ ] Upset
- [ ] Lost
- [ ] Angry
- [ ] Optimistic
- [ ] Creative
- [ ] Joyful
- [ ] Productive
- [ ] Bored
- [ ] Annoyed
- [ ] Confused
- [ ] Hesitant

Food Intake

Breakfast	Lunch	Dinner	Snacks

Blood Pressure Chart

Time	Systolic (Upper)	Diastolic (Lower)	Heart Rate

Medications

Three Goals for Today...

Notes

1. _______________________

2. _______________________

3. _______________________

What impacted your mood today?

What activities or people brought positivity to your day?

What thoughts or events made you feel anxious or upset today?

How did you cope with those feelings?

Did you practice self-care today? If not, what self-care activities can you plan for tomorrow?

Date: _____________   Day   M   T   W   T   F   S   S

Hours of Sleep: _____________

Mood (Morning)

Evening (Morning)

Water Intake	Energy Level

Did you feel any of the following today?

- [ ] Energized
- [ ] Happy
- [ ] Motivated
- [ ] Excited
- [ ] Sad
- [ ] Upset
- [ ] Lost
- [ ] Angry
- [ ] Optimistic
- [ ] Creative
- [ ] Joyful
- [ ] Productive
- [ ] Bored
- [ ] Annoyed
- [ ] Confused
- [ ] Hesitant

Food Intake

Breakfast	Lunch	Dinner	Snacks

Blood Pressure Chart

Time	Systolic (Upper)	Diastolic (Lower)	Heart Rate

Medications

Three Goals for Today...

1. ___________________________

2. ___________________________

3. ___________________________

Notes

What impacted your mood today?

What activities or people brought positivity to your day?

What thoughts or events made you feel anxious or upset today?

How did you cope with those feelings?

Did you practice self-care today? If not, what self-care activities can you plan for tomorrow?

Date: _________ Day   M   T   W   T   F   S   S

Hours of Sleep: _____________

Mood (Morning)

Evening (Morning)

Water Intake	Energy Level

Did you feel any of the following today?

- [ ] Energized
- [ ] Happy
- [ ] Motivated
- [ ] Excited
- [ ] Sad
- [ ] Upset
- [ ] Lost
- [ ] Angry
- [ ] Optimistic
- [ ] Creative
- [ ] Joyful
- [ ] Productive
- [ ] Bored
- [ ] Annoyed
- [ ] Confused
- [ ] Hesitant

Food Intake

Breakfast	Lunch	Dinner	Snacks

Blood Pressure Chart

Time	Systolic (Upper)	Diastolic (Lower)	Heart Rate

Medications

Three Goals for Today...

1.

2.

3.

Notes

What impacted your mood today?

What activities or people brought positivity to your day?

What thoughts or events made you feel anxious or upset today?

How did you cope with those feelings?

Did you practice self-care today? If not, what self-care activities can you plan for tomorrow?

Date: ___________   Day   M   T   W   T   F   S   S

Hours of Sleep: ___________

| | Water Intake | Energy Level |

Mood (Morning)

😄 🙂 😐 🙁 😠

Evening (Morning)

😄 🙂 😐 🙁 😠

Did you feel any of the following today?

- ☐ Energized
- ☐ Happy
- ☐ Motivated
- ☐ Excited
- ☐ Sad
- ☐ Upset
- ☐ Lost
- ☐ Angry
- ☐ Optimistic
- ☐ Creative
- ☐ Joyful
- ☐ Productive
- ☐ Bored
- ☐ Annoyed
- ☐ Confused
- ☐ Hesitant

Food Intake

Breakfast	Lunch	Dinner	Snacks

Blood Pressure Chart

Time	Systolic (Upper)	Diastolic (Lower)	Heart Rate

Medications

Three Goals for Today...

1.
2.
3.

Notes

What impacted your mood today?

What activities or people brought positivity to your day?

What thoughts or events made you feel anxious or upset today?

How did you cope with those feelings?

Did you practice self-care today? If not, what self-care activities can you plan for tomorrow?

Date: __________   Day   M   T   W   T   F   S   S

Hours of Sleep: __________

Mood (Morning)

Evening (Morning)

Water Intake | Energy Level

Did you feel any of the following today?

☐ Energized	☐ Happy	☐ Motivated	☐ Excited
☐ Sad	☐ Upset	☐ Lost	☐ Angry
☐ Optimistic	☐ Creative	☐ Joyful	☐ Productive
☐ Bored	☐ Annoyed	☐ Confused	☐ Hesitant

Food Intake

Breakfast	Lunch	Dinner	Snacks

Blood Pressure Chart

Time	Systolic (Upper)	Diastolic (Lower)	Heart Rate

Medications

Three Goals for Today...

Notes

1.

2.

3.

What impacted your mood today?

What activities or people brought positivity to your day?

What thoughts or events made you feel anxious or upset today?

How did you cope with those feelings?

Did you practice self-care today? If not, what self-care activities can you plan for tomorrow?

Date: ___________   Day   M   T   W   T   F   S   S

Hours of Sleep: ___________

Mood (Morning)

Evening (Morning)

Water Intake	Energy Level

Did you feel any of the following today?

- [ ] Energized
- [ ] Happy
- [ ] Motivated
- [ ] Excited
- [ ] Sad
- [ ] Upset
- [ ] Lost
- [ ] Angry
- [ ] Optimistic
- [ ] Creative
- [ ] Joyful
- [ ] Productive
- [ ] Bored
- [ ] Annoyed
- [ ] Confused
- [ ] Hesitant

Food Intake

Breakfast	Lunch	Dinner	Snacks

Blood Pressure Chart

Time	Systolic (Upper)	Diastolic (Lower)	Heart Rate

Medications

Three Goals for Today...

1.
2.
3.

Notes

What impacted your mood today?

What activities or people brought positivity to your day?

What thoughts or events made you feel anxious or upset today?

How did you cope with those feelings?

Did you practice self-care today? If not, what self-care activities can you plan for tomorrow?

Date: __________   Day   M   T   W   T   F   S   S

Hours of Sleep: __________

| Water Intake | Energy Level |

Mood (Morning)

Evening (Morning)

Did you feel any of the following today?

- ☐ Energized
- ☐ Happy
- ☐ Motivated
- ☐ Excited
- ☐ Sad
- ☐ Upset
- ☐ Lost
- ☐ Angry
- ☐ Optimistic
- ☐ Creative
- ☐ Joyful
- ☐ Productive
- ☐ Bored
- ☐ Annoyed
- ☐ Confused
- ☐ Hesitant

Food Intake

Breakfast	Lunch	Dinner	Snacks

Blood Pressure Chart

Time	Systolic (Upper)	Diastolic (Lower)	Heart Rate

Medications

Three Goals for Today...

1.

2.

3.

Notes

What impacted your mood today?

What activities or people brought positivity to your day?

What thoughts or events made you feel anxious or upset today?

How did you cope with those feelings?

Did you practice self-care today? If not, what self-care activities can you plan for tomorrow?

Date: _____________   Day   M   T   W   T   F   S   S

Hours of Sleep: _____________

Mood (Morning)

Water Intake | Energy Level

Evening (Morning)

Did you feel any of the following today?

- [ ] Energized
- [ ] Happy
- [ ] Motivated
- [ ] Excited
- [ ] Sad
- [ ] Upset
- [ ] Lost
- [ ] Angry
- [ ] Optimistic
- [ ] Creative
- [ ] Joyful
- [ ] Productive
- [ ] Bored
- [ ] Annoyed
- [ ] Confused
- [ ] Hesitant

Food Intake

Breakfast	Lunch	Dinner	Snacks

Blood Pressure Chart

Time	Systolic (Upper)	Diastolic (Lower)	Heart Rate

Medications

Three Goals for Today...   Notes

1. _____________________________

2. _____________________________

3. _____________________________

What impacted your mood today?

What activities or people brought positivity to your day?

What thoughts or events made you feel anxious or upset today?

How did you cope with those feelings?

Did you practice self-care today? If not, what self-care activities can you plan for tomorrow?

Date: _____________   Day   M   T   W   T   F   S   S

Hours of Sleep: _____________

Mood (Morning)

Evening (Morning)

Did you feel any of the following today?

- [ ] Energized
- [ ] Happy
- [ ] Motivated
- [ ] Excited
- [ ] Sad
- [ ] Upset
- [ ] Lost
- [ ] Angry
- [ ] Optimistic
- [ ] Creative
- [ ] Joyful
- [ ] Productive
- [ ] Bored
- [ ] Annoyed
- [ ] Confused
- [ ] Hesitant

Food Intake

Breakfast	Lunch	Dinner	Snacks

Blood Pressure Chart

Time	Systolic (Upper)	Diastolic (Lower)	Heart Rate

Medications

Three Goals for Today...

Notes

1.

2.

3.

What impacted your mood today?

What activities or people brought positivity to your day?

What thoughts or events made you feel anxious or upset today?

How did you cope with those feelings?

Did you practice self-care today? If not, what self-care activities can you plan for tomorrow?

Date: _____________   Day   M   T   W   T   F   S   S

Hours of Sleep: _____________

Mood (Morning)

Evening (Morning)

Did you feel any of the following today?

- [ ] Energized
- [ ] Happy
- [ ] Motivated
- [ ] Excited
- [ ] Sad
- [ ] Upset
- [ ] Lost
- [ ] Angry
- [ ] Optimistic
- [ ] Creative
- [ ] Joyful
- [ ] Productive
- [ ] Bored
- [ ] Annoyed
- [ ] Confused
- [ ] Hesitant

Food Intake

Breakfast	Lunch	Dinner	Snacks

Blood Pressure Chart

Time	Systolic (Upper)	Diastolic (Lower)	Heart Rate

Medications

Three Goals for Today...

1.
2.
3.

Notes

What impacted your mood today?

What activities or people brought positivity to your day?

What thoughts or events made you feel anxious or upset today?

How did you cope with those feelings?

Did you practice self-care today? If not, what self-care activities can you plan for tomorrow?

Date: _____________ Day M T W T F S S

Hours of Sleep: _____________

Mood (Morning)

Evening (Morning)

Water Intake

Energy Level

Did you feel any of the following today?

- [ ] Energized
- [ ] Happy
- [ ] Motivated
- [ ] Excited
- [ ] Sad
- [ ] Upset
- [ ] Lost
- [ ] Angry
- [ ] Optimistic
- [ ] Creative
- [ ] Joyful
- [ ] Productive
- [ ] Bored
- [ ] Annoyed
- [ ] Confused
- [ ] Hesitant

Food Intake

Breakfast	Lunch	Dinner	Snacks

Blood Pressure Chart

Time	Systolic (Upper)	Diastolic (Lower)	Heart Rate

Medications

Three Goals for Today...

1.

2.

3.

Notes

What impacted your mood today?

What activities or people brought positivity to your day?

What thoughts or events made you feel anxious or upset today?

How did you cope with those feelings?

Did you practice self-care today? If not, what self-care activities can you plan for tomorrow?

Date: ___________   Day   M   T   W   T   F   S   S

Hours of Sleep: ___________

| Water Intake | Energy Level |

Mood (Morning)

Evening (Morning)

Did you feel any of the following today?

- ☐ Energized
- ☐ Happy
- ☐ Motivated
- ☐ Excited
- ☐ Sad
- ☐ Upset
- ☐ Lost
- ☐ Angry
- ☐ Optimistic
- ☐ Creative
- ☐ Joyful
- ☐ Productive
- ☐ Bored
- ☐ Annoyed
- ☐ Confused
- ☐ Hesitant

Food Intake

Breakfast	Lunch	Dinner	Snacks

Blood Pressure Chart

Time	Systolic (Upper)	Diastolic (Lower)	Heart Rate

Medications

Three Goals for Today...

Notes

1. _______________________

2. _______________________

3. _______________________

What impacted your mood today?

What activities or people brought positivity to your day?

What thoughts or events made you feel anxious or upset today?

How did you cope with those feelings?

Did you practice self-care today? If not, what self-care activities can you plan for tomorrow?

Date: _________   Day   M   T   W   T   F   S   S

Hours of Sleep: _________

Mood (Morning)

Evening (Morning)

| Water Intake | Energy Level |

Did you feel any of the following today?

☐ Energized	☐ Happy	☐ Motivated	☐ Excited
☐ Sad	☐ Upset	☐ Lost	☐ Angry
☐ Optimistic	☐ Creative	☐ Joyful	☐ Productive
☐ Bored	☐ Annoyed	☐ Confused	☐ Hesitant

Food Intake

Breakfast	Lunch	Dinner	Snacks

Blood Pressure Chart

Time	Systolic (Upper)	Diastolic (Lower)	Heart Rate

Medications

Three Goals for Today...

Notes

1. ___________________

2. ___________________

3. ___________________

What impacted your mood today?

What activities or people brought positivity to your day?

What thoughts or events made you feel anxious or upset today?

How did you cope with those feelings?

Did you practice self-care today? If not, what self-care activities can you plan for tomorrow?